At Home with Books

A Family Reading Partnership Book

written and illustrated
by Katrina Morse

Text and illustrations copyright ©2007 by Katrina Morse

Family Reading Partnership
54 Gunderman Rd., Ithaca, NY 14850

Family Reading
Partnership
www.familyreading.org

Text of this book is set in Gill Sans and Billy Regular.
Illustrations are rendered in acrylic paint and colored pencil.

ISBN-13: 978-0-9846414-2-0

Welcome to the
Bear Family's home!

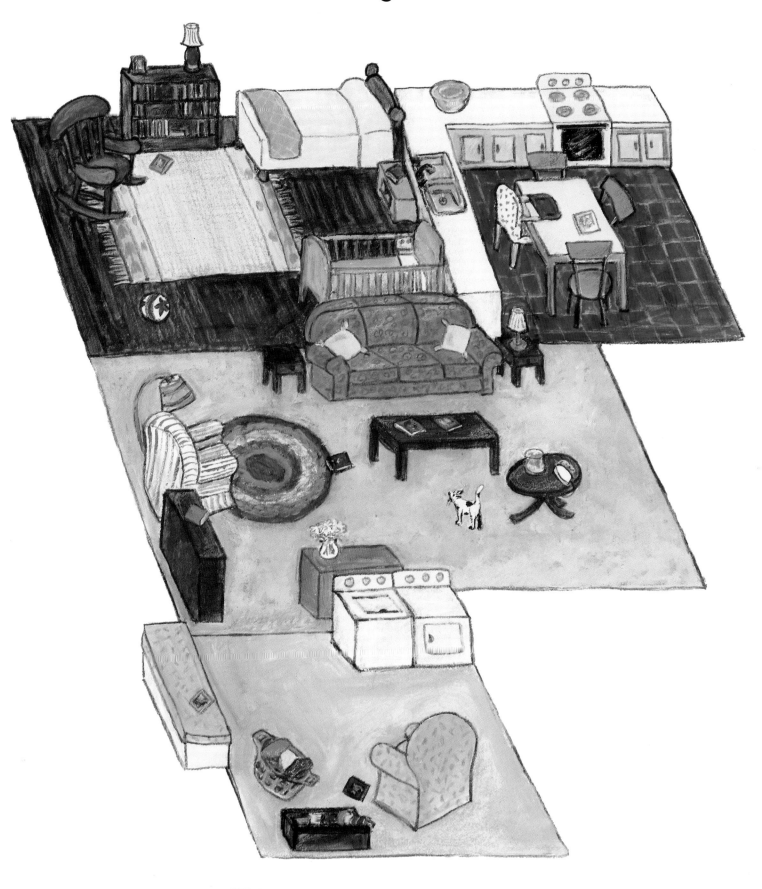

Daddy reads to my sister and me
every single day.

As the sun comes up we read in the
creaky red rocking chair, book after book.

I like to show Daddy my favorite parts of the story.

"Look Daddy! This is where the brave giant finds the blue dragon!"

When the giant walked to the cast.

was surprised to see a dragon blocking the way.

We read before breakfast
while pancakes are cooking,
book after book.

I like it when Daddy makes all the noises in the story.

In a big voice he says, "Wooo, wooo!"

Then he reads, "The train chugged slowly up the rocky mountain."

Mommy reads to us every day, too.

We read in a bright, warm sunbeam,
book after book.

I pick a story about kittens because we have one of our own.

Kitty ate her cat food and walked across the floor.
Soon she was walking right out the door.

"Mommy, that looks like Patches—even the spot on her forehead!"

We make a big nest out of blankets and read in it, book after book.

I like my book from the library because it tells me new things.

When I hear Mommy read, "In winter, frogs sleep in mud at the bottom of a pond," I want to know more.

Grandma reads to us
when she comes to visit.

We read on a
round, flowered pillow
in the playroom,
book after book.

I like it when Grandma reads stories with silly sounds.

I laugh when she reads...

Uncle reads to us, too.
He sits in his favorite
striped chair and we listen to
book after book.

He reads the same book
again and again.
I say, "I love this book,"
and Uncle says,
"I love it, too!"

When our friend
comes to see us,
we all read together.

We read
snuggled up
on the big, soft sofa,
book after book.

Our friend says, "Let's guess what happens next."
"I think the butterflies are going to
do a jungle dance,"
I tell her.

A beautiful red parrot glides high in the air ove
the rushing river.

Down at the water, delicate yellow butterflies gather on a rock.

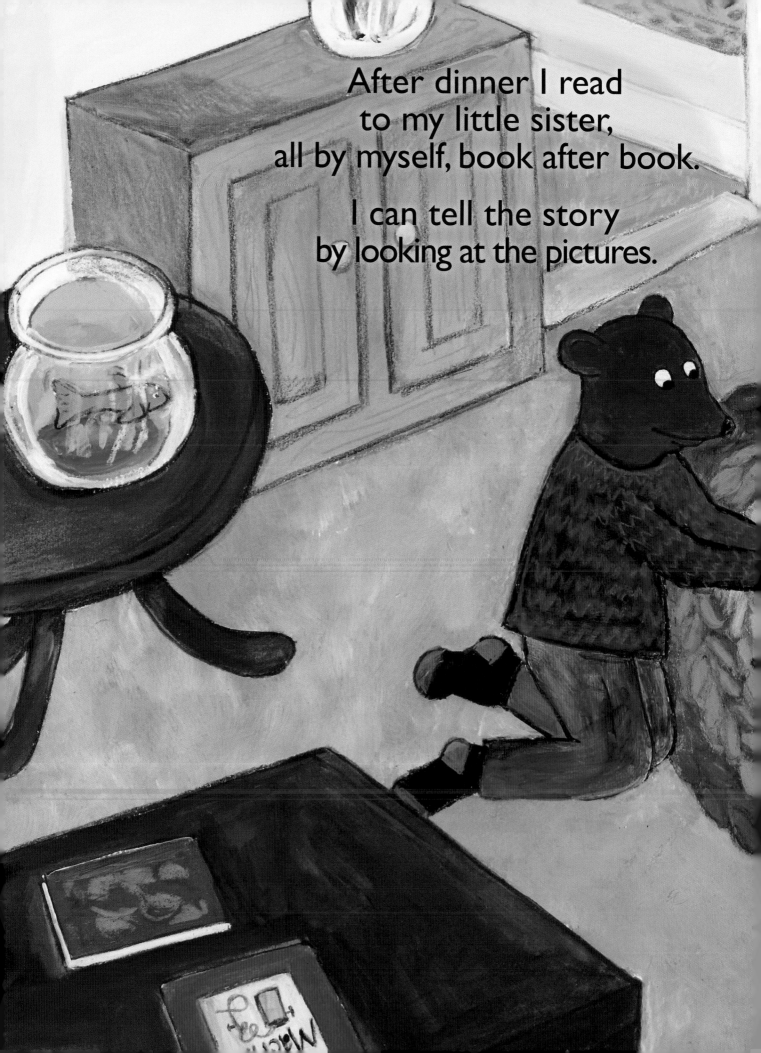

After dinner I read
to my little sister,
all by myself, book after book.

I can tell the story
by looking at the pictures.

"Clap your hands
like a seal," I say,
and my sister and I
both clap!

My favorite time to hear a story is at the end of the day.

We listen in our cozy beds,
covers tucked up to our chins,
book after book
after book.

"Good night, dear ones.
We'll read more books
tomorrow."

Reading aloud is fun
for you and your child
when you remember to play.

Wooo Wooo

Play with the words; read softer,
louder, faster, s-l-o-w-e-r.
Roar, whisper, laugh, or splutter.

Play with the pictures—play a game of
I spy, I think, I guess, what's next?

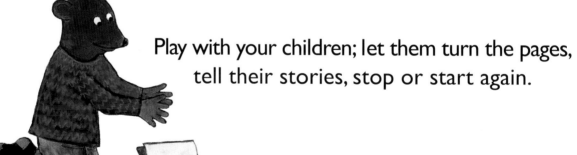

Play with your children; let them turn the pages,
tell their stories, stop or start again.

Read for fun every day!

Ideas to Help Raise a Child Who is... At Home with Books!

Make Reading and Talking Part of Your Everyday Family Life

- Begin sharing books with your child at birth... and never stop.
- Find times to read throughout the day (at breakfast? after a nap?)
- Tell stories that you remember from your childhood or a story you make up.
- Ask your child questions– "why," "how," or "what do you think?"
- Pack books to take along in the car, on the bus, or to appointments in case there's a wait.
- Play with words and language—make up silly rhymes or change a story's ending.
- Ask your child to retell the story in their own words or "read" to you by looking at the pictures.

Help Your Child Fall in Love with Books

- Make a special cozy place to snuggle up and read.
- Let your child choose the book, hold it, and turn the pages.
- Read your child's favorite book over and over if he or she asks.
- Make noises that are in the story and special voices for each character.
- Read books with rhyme or repeated phrases, pause before you finish a line, and let your child fill in the words.

Fill Your Home with Books and Reading Fun

- Visit the library often.
- Find books to keep for your child's collection at yard sales or trade books with friends.
- Keep books in small boxes or baskets in different parts of your home so there are always books close at hand for your child.
- Let your child see you read–books, newspapers, cookbooks, magazines.
- Make your own books with pictures that your child draws or cuts from magazines and add your child's words.

Start Family Reading Traditions

- Show your child that books are special by including books as gifts for birthdays, holidays, and special occasions.
- Welcome new babies with a special book and a note inside.
- Have special *At Home with Books* nights when screens are turned off and everyone reads!

About Family Reading Partnership

Family Reading Partnership is a national leader in community literacy efforts, promoting and supporting family, school, and community engagement around children's books to create a culture of literacy in every home.

At Home With Books is one of many Family Reading Partnership initiatives designed to deepen and strengthen the connection children and families have with books—building not only the foundation for reading, but the foundation for a good life.

For more information visit: **www.familyreading.org**

About the Author/Illustrator

Katrina Morse likes to paint, create, write, explore, and dance. She lives in Ithaca, New York, where the beauty and diversity of the people and the natural world inspire her imagination.

To learn more about Katrina's children's books, book activities for kids, parents, and teachers, or schedule a visit to your school or library visit: **www.katrinamorse.com**

At Home with Books/En Casa con Libros

English & Spanish bilingual edition!

"At Home with Books/En Casa con Libros" es una de las muchas iniciativas del Family Reading Partnership – diseñada para profundizar y reforzar la conexión que tienen los niños y familias con libros – creando no solo una fundación para la lectura, si no también para una buena vida.

Order at: **www.familyreading.org**